THE DEVIL

IF THE DEVIL SHOULD DIE WOULD GOD MAKE ANOTHER?

First Edition 1899
Robert Ingersoll

New Edition 2019
Edited by Tarl Warwick

COPYRIGHT AND DISCLAIMER

FOREWORD

This little work is technically a lengthy speech more than a book in and of itself. The creator, Robert Ingersoll, was not only one of the primary orators of his era, but also a formidable philosophical champion of irreligion and skepticism towards the spiritual. This particular text then is predominantly a lengthy refutation of the concept of a Devil, of Hell, and of similar facets of what was then accepted orthodox Christendom.

Indeed, some of the ideas expressed by the agnostic Ingersoll now find themselves in part adopted even by some religious groups now in the era of modern liberalism- with the Unitarians, particularly, among others, and in the more "progressive" offshoots of a half dozen other religious orders as well, being increasingly adopted as science pushes against and, generally, defeats, the more fantastical side of religion.

In part this tract is logical in nature, pointing to contradictory or odd elements especially of the New Testament, such as the admission of lesser demons that Jesus was the messiah while Satan, supposedly, was ignorant of this and genuinely believed himself to have the ability to tempt or subjugate the Son of God. The other part is ethical and emotional and particularly at the end this is dwelt upon in some degree of depth- the injustice, per se, of a Hell existing at all.

This edition of "The Devil" has been carefully edited and reformatted from the original. Care has been taken to retain all original intent and meaning.

THE DEVIL

A little while ago I delivered a lecture on 'Superstition,' in which, among other things, I said that the Christian world could not deny the existence of the Devil; that the Devil was really the keystone of the arch, and that to take him away was to destroy the entire system. A great many clergymen answered or criticized this statement. Some of these ministers avowed their belief in the existence of his Satanic Majesty, while others actually denied his existence; but some, without stating their own position, said that others believed, not in the existence of a personal devil, but in the personification of evil, and that all references to the Devil in the Scriptures could be explained on the hypothesis that the Devil thus alluded to was simply a personification of evil.

When I read these answers I thought of this line from Heine: "Christ rode on an ass, but now asses ride on Christ."

Now, the questions are, first, whether the Devil does really exist; second, whether the sacred Scriptures teach the existence of the Devil and of unclean spirits, and third, whether this belief in devils is a necessary part of what is known as "orthodox Christianity."

Now, where did the idea that a Devil exists come from? How was it produced? Fear is an artist- a sculptor- a painter. All tribes and nations, having suffered, having been the sport and prey of natural phenomena, having been struck by lightning, poisoned by weeds, overwhelmed by volcanoes, destroyed by earthquakes, believed in the existence of a Devil, who was the king- the ruler- of innumerable smaller devils, and all these devils have been from time immemorial regarded as the enemies of men.

THE DEVIL

Along the banks of the Ganges wandered the Asuras, the most powerful of evil spirits. Their business was to war against the Devas- that is to say, the gods- and at the same time against human beings. There, too, were the ogres, the Jakshas and many others who killed and devoured human beings. The Persians turned this around, and with them the Asuras were good and the Devas bad. Ormuzd was the good- the god- Ahriman the evil- the devil- and between the god and the devil was waged a perpetual war. Some of the Persians thought that the evil would finally triumph, but others insisted that the good would be the victor.

In Egypt the devil was Set- or, as usually called, Typhon- and the good god was Osiris. Set and his legions fought against Osiris and against the human race. Among the Greeks, the Titans were the enemies of the gods. Ate was the spirit that tempted, and such was her power that at one time she tempted and misled the god of gods, even Zeus himself. These ideas about gods and devils often changed, because in the days of Socrates a demon was not a devil, but a guardian angel. We obtain our Devil from the Jews, and they got him from Babylon. The Jews cultivated the science of Demonology, and at one time it was believed that there were nine kinds of demons; Beelzebub, prince of the false gods of the other nations; the Pythian Apollo, prince of liars; Belial, prince of mischief makers; Asmodeus, prince of revengeful devils; Satan, prince of witches and magicians; Meresin, prince of aerial devils, who caused thunderstorms and plagues; Abaddon, who caused wars, tumults and combustions; Diabolus, who drives to despair, and Mammon, prince of the tempters.

It was believed that demons and sorcerers frequently came together and held what were called 'Sabbats;' that is to say, orgies. It was also known that sorcerers and witches had marks on their bodies that had been imprinted by the Devil. Of course these devils were all made by the people, and in these devils we find the prejudices of their makers. The Europeans always represent their devils as black, while the Africans believed that theirs were white. So it was believed that people by the aid of the Devil could assume any shape that they wished. Witches and wizards were changed into wolves, dogs, cats and serpents. This change to animal form was exceedingly common.

Within two years, between 1598 and 1600, in one district of France, the district of Jura, more than six hundred men and women were tried and convicted before one judge of having changed themselves into wolves, and all were put to death. This is only one instance. There are thousands. There is no time to give the history of this belief in devils. It has been universal. The consequences have been terrible beyond the imagination. Millions and millions of men, women and children, of fathers and mothers, have been sacrificed upon the altar of this ignorant and idiotic belief. Of course, the Christians of to-day do not believe that the devils of the Hindus, Egyptians, Persians or Babylonians existed. They think that those nations created their own devils, precisely the same as they did their own gods. But the Christians of today admit that for many centuries Christians did believe in the existence of countless devils; that the Fathers of the Church believed as sincerely in the Devil and his demons as in God and his angels ; that they were just as sure about hell as heaven.

I admit that people did the best they could to account for what they saw, for what they experienced. I admit that the devils as well as the gods were naturally produced- the effect of nature upon then human brain. The cause of phenomena filled our ancestors not only with wonder, but with terror. The miraculous, the supernatural, was not only believed in, but was always expected. A man walking in the woods at night- just a glimmering of the moon- everything uncertain and shadowy- sees a monstrous form. One arm is raised. His blood grows cold, his hair lifts. In the gloom he sees the eyes of an ogre; eyes that flame with malice.

He feels that the something is approaching. He turns, and with a cry of horror takes to his heels. He is afraid to look back. Spent, out of breath, shaking with fear, he reaches his hut and falls at the door. When he regains consciousness, he tells his story and, of course, the children believe. When they become men and women they tell father's story of having seen the Devil to their children, and so the children and grandchildren not only believe, but think they know, that their father- their grandfather- actually saw a devil.

An old woman sitting by the fire at night- a storm raging without- hears the mournful sough of the wind. To her it becomes a voice. Her imagination is touched, and the voice seems to utter words. Out of these words she constructs a message or a warning from the unseen world. If the words are good, she has heard an angel; if they are threatening and malicious, she has heard a devil. She tells this to her children and they believe. They say that mother's religion is good enough for them. A girl suffering from hysteria falls into a trance- has visions of the infernal world. The priest sprinkles holy water on her pallid face, saying: "She hath a devil." A man utters a terrible cry; falls to the ground, foam and blood issue from his mouth, his limbs are convulsed. The spectators say "This is the Devil's work."

Through all the ages people have mistaken dreams and visions of fear for realities. To them the insane were inspired; epileptics were possessed by devils; apoplexy was the work of an unclean spirit. For many centuries people believed that they had actually seen the malicious phantoms of the night, and so thorough was this belief- so vivid- that they made pictures of them. They knew how they looked. They drew and chiseled their hoofs, their horns- all their malicious deformities.

Now, I admit that all these monsters were naturally produced. The people believed that hell was their native land; that the Devil was a king, and that he and his imps waged war against the children of men. Curiously enough some of these devils were made out of degraded gods, and, naturally enough, many devils were made out of the gods of other nations. So that frequently the gods of one people were the devils of another.

In nature there are opposing forces. Some of the forces work for what man calls good; some for what he calls evil. Back of these forces our ancestors put will, intelligence and design. They could not believe that the good and evil came from the same being. So back of the good they put God; back of the evil, the Devil.

THE DEVIL

II: THE ATLAS OF CHRISTIANITY IS THE DEVIL

the religion known as 'Christianity' was invented by God himself to repair in part the wreck and ruin that had resulted from the Devil's work. Take the Devil from the scheme of salvation- from the atonement- from the dogma of eternal pain- and the foundation is gone.

The Devil is the keystone of the arch. He inflicted the wounds that Christ came to heal. He corrupted the human race. The question now is; Does the Old Testament teach the existence of the Devil? If the Old Testament teaches anything, it does teach the existence of the Devil, of Satan, of the Serpent, of the enemy of God and man, the deceiver of men and women. Those who believe the Scriptures are compelled to say that this Devil was created by God, and that God knew when he created him just what he would do- the exact measure of his success; knew that he would be a successful rival; knew that he would deceive and corrupt the children of men; knew that, by reason of this Devil, countless millions of human beings would suffer eternal torment in the prison of pain. And this God also knew when he created the Devil; that he, God, would be compelled to leave his throne, to be born a babe in Palestine, and to suffer a cruel death. All this he knew when he created the Devil. Why did he create him?

It is no answer to say that this Devil was once an angel of light and fell from his high estate because he was free. God knew what he would do with his freedom when he made him and gave him liberty of action, and as a matter of fact must have made him with the intention that he should rebel; that he should fall; that he should become a devil; that he should tempt and corrupt the father and mother of the human race; that he should make hell a necessity, and that, in consequence of his creation,

9

countless millions of the children of men would suffer eternal pain. Why did he create him? Admit that God is infinitely wise. Has he ingenuity enough, to frame an excuse for the creation of the Devil?

Does the Old Testament teach the existence of a real, living Devil?

The first account of this being is found in Genesis, and in that account he is called the 'Serpent.' He is declared to have been more subtle than any beast of the field. According to the account, this Serpent had a conversation with Eve, the first woman. We are not told in what language they conversed, or how they understood each other, as this was the first time they had met. Where did Eve get her language? Where did the Serpent get his? Of course, such questions are impudent, but at the same time they are natural. The result of this conversation was that Eve ate the forbidden fruit and induced Adam to do the same. This is what is called the 'Fall,' and for this they were expelled from the Garden of Eden. On account of this, God cursed the earth with weeds and thorns and brambles, cursed man with toil, made woman a slave, and cursed maternity with pain and sorrow.

How men- good men- can worship this God; how women- good women- can love this Jehovah, is beyond my imagination. In addition to the other curses the Serpent was cursed- condemned to crawl on his belly and to eat dust. Wc do not know by what means, before that time, he moved from place to place- whether he walked or flew; neither do we know on what food he lived- all we know is that after that time he crawled and lived on dust. Jehovah told him that this he should do all the days of his life. It would seem from this that the Serpent was not at that time immortal- that there was somewhere in the future a milepost at which the life of this Serpent stopped.

THE DEVIL

Whether he is living yet or not, I am not certain. It will not do to say that this is allegory, or a poem, because this proves too much. If the Serpent did not in fact exist, how do we know that Adam and Eve existed? Is all that is said about God allegory, and poetic, or mythical? Is the whole account, after all, an ignorant dream? Neither will it do to say that the Devil- the Serpent- was a personification of evil. Do personifications of evil talk? Can a personification of evil crawl on its belly? Can a personification of evil eat dust?

If we say that the Devil was a personification of evil, are we not at the same time compelled to say that Jehovah was a personification of good ; that the Garden of Eden was the personification of a place, and that the whole story is a personification of something that did not happen? Maybe that Adam and Eve were not driven out of the Garden; they may have suffered only the personification of exile. And maybe the cherubim placed at the gate of Eden, with flaming swords, were only personifications of policemen. There is no escape. If the Old Testament is true, the Devil does exist, and it is impossible to explain him away without at the same time explaining God away. So there are many references to devils, and spirits of divination and of evil which I have not the time to call attention to; but, in the Book of Job, Satan, the Devil has a conversation with God. It is this Devil that brings the sorrows and losses on the upright man. It is this Devil that raises the storm that wrecks the Homes of Job's children. It is this Devil that kills the children of Job. Take this Devil from that book, and all meaning, plot and purpose fade away.

Is it possible to say that the Devil in Job was only a personification of evil? In Chronicles we are told that Satan provoked David to number Israel. For this act of David, caused by the Devil, God did not smite the Devil, did not punish David, but he killed 70,000 poor innocent Jews who had done nothing but stand up and be counted. Was this Devil who tempted David a personification of evil, or was Jehovah a personification of the devilish? In Zachariah we are told that Joshua stood before the angel of the Lord, and that Satan stood at his right hand to resist him, and that the Lord rebuked Satan.

If words convey any meaning, the Old Testament teaches the existence of the Devil. All the passages about witches and those having familiar spirits were born of a belief in the Devil. When a man who loved Jehovah wanted revenge on his enemy he fell on his holy knees, and from a heart full of religion he cried: 'Let Satan stand at his right hand.'

THE DEVIL

III: TAKE THE DEVIL FROM THE DRAMA OF CHRISTIANITY AND THE PLOT IS GONE

The next question is: Does the New Testament teach the existence of the Devil? As a matter of fact, the New Testament is far more explicit than the Old. The Jews, believing that Jehovah was God, had very little business for a devil. Jehovah was wicked enough and malicious enough to take the Devil's place. The first reference in the New Testament to the Devil is in the fourth chapter of Matthew. We are told that Jesus was led by the Spirit into the wilderness to be tempted of the Devil. It seems that he was not led by the Devil into the wilderness, but by the Spirit ; that the Spirit and the Devil were acting together in a kind of pious conspiracy. In the wilderness Jesus fasted forty days, and then the Devil asked him to turn stones into bread. The Devil also took him to Jerusalem and set him on a pinnacle of the temple, and tried to induce him to leap to the earth. The Devil also took him to the top of a mountain and showed him all the kingdoms of the world and offered them all to him in exchange for his worship. Jesus refused. The Devil went away and angels came and ministered to Christ. Now, the question is: Did the author of this account believe in the existence of the Devil, or did he regard this Devil as a personification of evil, and did he intend that his account should be understood as an allegory, or as a poem, or as a myth.

Was Jesus tempted? If he was tempted, who tempted him? Did anybody offer him the kingdoms of the world? Did the writer of the account try to convey to the reader the thought that Christ was tempted by the Devil? If Christ was not tempted by the Devil, then the temptation was born in his own heart. If that be true, can it be said that he was divine? If these adders, these vipers, were coiled in his bosom, was he the son of God? Was he pure?

13

THE DEVIL

In the same chapter we are told that Christ healed "those which were possessed of devils, and those which, were lunatic, and those that had the palsy."

From this it is evident that a distinction was made between those possessed with devils and those whose minds were affected and those who were afflicted with diseases. In the eighth chapter we are told that people brought unto Christ many that were possessed with devils, and that he cast out the spirits with his word. Now, can we say that these people were possessed with personifications of evil, and that these personifications of evil were cast out? Are these personifications entities? Have they form and shape? Do they occupy space? Then comes the story of the two men possessed with devils who came from the tombs, and were exceeding fierce. It is said that when they saw Jesus they cried out: "What have we to do with thee, Jesus, thou Son of God? Art thou come hither to torment us before the time?" If these were simply personifications of evil, how did they know that Jesus was the Son of God, and how can a personification of evil be tormented?

We are told that at the same time, a good way off, many swine were feeding, and that the devils besought Christ, saying: "If thou cast us out, suffer us to go away into the herd of swine." And he said unto them: "Go." Is it possible that personifications of evil would desire to enter the bodies of swine, and is it possible that it was necessary for them to have the consent of Christ before they could enter the swine? The question naturally arises : How did they enter into the body of the man? Did they do that without Christ's consent, and is it a fact that Christ protects swine and neglects human beings? Can personifications have desires?

In the ninth chapter of Matthew there was a dumb man brought to Jesus, possessed with a devil. Jesus cast out the devil and the dumb man spake. Did a personification of evil prevent the dumb man from talking? Did it in some way paralyze his organs of speech? Could it have done this had it only been a personification of evil? In the tenth chapter Jesus gives his twelve disciples power to cast out unclean spirits. What were unclean spirits supposed to be? Did they really exist? Were they shadows, impersonations, allegories? When Jesus sent his disciples forth on the great mission to convert the world, among other things he told them to heal the sick, to raise the dead and to cast out devils. Here a distinction is made between the sick and those who were possessed by evil spirits. Now, what did Christ mean by devils?

In the twelfth chapter we are told of a very remarkable case. There was brought unto Jesus one possessed with a devil, blind and dumb, and Jesus healed him. The blind and dumb both spake and saw. Thereupon the Pharisees said: "This fellow doth not cast out devils but by Beelzebub, the prince of devils." Jesus answered by saying: "Every kingdom divided against itself is brought to desolation. If Satan cast out Satan, he is divided against himself."

Why did not Christ tell the Pharisees that he did not cast out devils- only personifications of evil, and that with these personifications Beelzebub had nothing to do? Another question: Did the Pharisees believe in the existence of devils, or had they the personification idea?

At the same time Christ said: "If I cast out devils by the Spirit of God, then the kingdom of God is come unto you."

If he meant anything by these words he certainly intended to convey the idea that what he did demonstrated the superiority of God over the Devil. Did Christ believe in the existence of the Devil? In the fifteenth chapter is the account of the woman of Canaan who cried unto Jesus, saying: "Have mercy on me, O Lord, thou son of David. My daughter is sorely vexed with a devil." On account of her faith Christ made the daughter whole. In the sixteenth chapter a man brought his son to Jesus. The boy was a lunatic, sore vexed, oftentimes falling in the fire and water. The disciples had tried to cure him and had failed. Jesus rebuked the devil, and the devil departed out of him and the boy was cured. Was the devil in this case a personification of evil? The disciples then asked Jesus why they could not cast that devil out. Jesus told them that it was because of their unbelief, and then added: "Howbeit this kind goeth not out but by prayer and fasting."

From this it would seem that some personifications were easier to expel than others. The first chapter of Mark throws a little light on the story of the temptation of Christ. Matthew tells us that Jesus was led up of the Spirit into the wilderness to be tempted of the Devil. In Mark we are told who this Spirit was:

"And straightway coming up out of the water he saw the heavens opened, and the Spirit like a dove descending upon him. And there came a voice from heaven, saying: 'Thou art my beloved Son, in whom I am well pleased.' And immediately the Spirit driveth him into the wilderness."

Why the Holy Ghost should hand Christ over to the tender mercies of the Devil is not explained. And it is all the more wonderful when we remember that the Holy Ghost was the third person in the Trinity and Christ the second, and that this Holy Ghost was, in fact, God, and that Christ also was, in fact, God, so that God led God into the wilderness to be tempted of the Devil.

We are told that Christ was in the wilderness forty days tempted of Satan, and was with the wild beasts, and that the angels ministered unto him. Were these angels real angels, or were they personifications of good, of comfort?

So we see that the same Spirit that came out of heaven, the same Spirit that said 'This is my beloved son,' drove Christ into the wilderness to be tempted of Satan. Was this Devil a real being? Was this Spirit who claimed to be the father of Christ a real being, or was he a personification? Are the heavens a real place? Are they a personification? Did the wild beasts live and did the angels minister into Christ? In other words, is the story true, or is it poetry, or metaphor, or mistake, or falsehood?

It might be asked: Why did God wish to be tempted by the Devil? Was God's ambition to obtain a victory over Satan? Was Satan foolish enough to think that he could mislead God, and is it possible that the Devil offered to give the world as a bribe to its creator and owner, knowing at the same time that Christ was the creator and owner, and also knowing that he (Christ) knew that he (the Devil) knew that he (Christ) was the creator and owner? Is not the whole story absurdly idiotic? The Devil knew that Christ was God, and knew that Christ knew that the tempter was the Devil. It may be asked how I know that the Devil knew that Christ was God. My answer is found in the same chapter. There is an account of what a devil said to Christ:

"Let us alone. What have we to do with thee, thou Jesus of Nazareth? Art thou come to destroy us? I know thee. Thou art the holy one of God."

Certainly, if the little devils knew this, the Devil himself must have had like information. Jesus rebuked this devil and said to him; "Hold thy peace, and come out of him." And when the unclean spirit had torn him and cried with a loud voice, he came out of him. So we are told that Jesus cast out many devils, and suffered not the devils to speak because they knew him. So it is said in the third chapter that "unclean spirits, when they saw him, fell down before him and cried, saying, 'Thou art the son of God.'"

In the fifth chapter is an account of casting out the devils that went into the swine, and we are told that "all the devils besought him saying, 'Send us into the swine,' And Jesus gave them leave." Again I ask: Was it necessary for the devils to get the permission of Christ before they could enter swine? Again I ask: By whose permission did they enter into the man?

Could personifications of evil enter a herd of swine, or could personifications of evil make a bargain with Christ? In the sixth chapter we are told that the disciples "cast out many devils and anointed with oil many that were sick." Here again the distinction is made between those possessed by devils and those afflicted by disease. It will not do to say that the devils were diseases or personifications. In the seventh chapter a Greek woman whose daughter was possessed by a devil besought Christ to cast this devil out. At last Christ said: "The devil is gone out of thy daughter."

In the ninth chapter one of the multitnde said unto Christ: "I have brought unto thee my son which hath a dumb spirit. I spoke unto thy disciples that they should cast him out, and they could not." So they brought this boy before Christ, and when the boy saw him, the spirit tare him, and he fell on the ground and "wallowed, foaming."

Christ asked the father: "How long is it ago since this came unto him?" And he answered: "Of a child, and ofttimes it hath cast him into the fire and into the waters to destroy him."

Then Christ said: "Thou dumb and deaf spirit, I charge thee, come out of him, and enter no more into him."

18

THE DEVIL

And the spirit cried, and rent him sore, and came out of him; and he was as one dead; insomuch that many said, 'He is dead.' Then the disciples asked Jesus why they could not cast them out, and Jesus said: "This kind can come forth by nothing but by prayer and fasting." Is there any doubt about the belief of the man who wrote this account? Is there any allegory, or poetry, or myth in this story? The devil, in this case, was not an ordinary, every-day devil. He was dumb and deaf; it was no use to order him out, because he could not hear. The only way was to pray and fast.

Is there such a thing as a dumb and deaf devil? If so, the devils must be organized. They must have ears and organs of speech, and they must be dumb because there is something the matter with the apparatus of speaking, and they must be deaf because something is the matter with their ears. It would seem from this that they are not simply spiritual beings, but organized on a physical basis. Now, we know that the ears do not hear. It is the brain that hears. So these devils must have brains; that is to say, they must have been what we call "organized beings."

Now, it is hardly possible that personifications of evil are dumb or deaf. That is to say, that they have physical imperfections. In the same chapter John tells Christ that he saw one casting out devils in Christ's name who did not follow with them, and Jesus said; "Forbid him not." By this he seemed to admit that some one, not a follower of his, was casting out devils in his name. and he was willing that he should go on, because, as he said; "For there is no man which shall do a miracle in my name that can lightly speak evil of me."

In the fourth chapter of Luke the story of the temptation of Christ by the Devil is again told with a few additions. All the writers, having been inspired, did not remember exactly the same things. Luke tells us that the Devil said unto Christ, having shown him all the kingdoms of the world in a moment of time: "All this power will I give thee and the glory of them, for that is delivered unto me, and to whomsoever I will I give it. If thou wilt worship me, all shall be thine."

We are also told that when the Devil had ended all the temptation he departed from him for a season. The date of his return is not given. In the same chapter we are told that a man in the synagogue had a "spirit of an unclean devil." This devil recognized Jesus and admitted that he was the Holy One of God. As a matter of fact, the Apostles seemed to have relied upon the evidence of devils to substantiate the divinity of their Lord. Jesus said to this devil: "Hold thy peace and come out of him." And the devil, after throwing the man down, came out. In the forty-first verse of the same chapter it is said: "And devils also came out of many, crying out and saying, 'Thou art Christ, the Son of God.'"

It is also said that Christ rebuked them and suffered them not to speak, for they knew that he was Christ. Now, it will not do to say that these devils were diseases, because diseases could not talk, and diseases would not recognize Christ as the Son of God. After all, epilepsy is not a theologian. I admit that lunacy comes nearer. In the eighth chapter is told again the story of the devils and the swine. In this account, Jesus asked the devil his name, and the devil replied 'Legion.'

In the ninth chapter is told the story of the devil that the disciples could not cast out, but was cast out by Christ, and in the thirteenth chapter it is said that the Pharisees came to Jesus, telling him to go away, because Herod would kill him, and Jesus said unto these Pharisees; "Go ye, and tell that fox, behold, I cast out devils." What did lie mean by this ? Did He mean that lie cured diseases? No. Because in the same sentence he says, "And I do cures today," making a distinction between devils and diseases. In the twenty-second chapter an account of the betrayal of Christ by Judas is given in these words: "Then entered Satan into Judas Iscariot, being of the number of the twelve. And he went his way and communed with the chief priests and captains how he might betray him unto them. And they were glad, and covenanted to give him money."

According to Christ the little devils knew that he was the Son of God. Certainly, then, Satan, king of all the fiends, knew that Christ was divine. And he not only knew that, but he knew all about the scheme of salvation. He knew that Christ wished to make an atonement of blood by the sacrifice of himself. According to Christian theologians, the Devil has always done his utmost to gain possession of the souls of men. At the time he entered into Judas, persuading him to betray Christ, he knew that if Christ was betrayed he would be crucified, and that he would make an atonement for all believers, and that, as a result, he, the Devil, would lose all the souls that Christ gained. What interest had the Devil in defeating himself? If he could have prevented the betrayal, then Christ would not have been crucified. No atonement would have been made, and the whole world would have gone to hell. The success of the Devil would have been complete. But, according to this story, the Devil outwitted himself. How thankful we should be to his Satanic Majesty. He opened for us the gates of paradise and made it possible for us to obtain eternal life. Without Satan, without Judas, not a single human being could have become an angel of light. All would have been wingless devils in the prison of flame. In Jerusalem, to the extent of his power, Satan repaired the wreck and ruin he had wrought in the Garden of Eden.

Certainly the writers of the New Testament believed in the existence of the Devil. In the eighth chapter it is said that out of Mary Magdalene were cast seven devils. To me Mary Magdalene is the most beautiful character in the New Testament.

THE DEVIL

She is the one true disciple. In the darkness of the crucifixion she lingered near. She was the first at the sepulcher. Defeat, disaster, disgrace, could not conquer her love. And yet, according to the account, when she met the risen Christ, he said: 'Touch me not.' This was the reward of her infinite devotion.

In the Gospel of John we are told that John the Baptist said that he saw the Spirit descending from heaven like a dove, and that it abode upon Christ. But in the Gospel of John nothing is said about the Spirit driving Christ into the wilderness to be tempted by the Devil. Possibly John never heard of that, or forgot it, or did not believe it. But in the thirteenth chapter I find this: "And supper being ended, the Devil having now put into the heart of Judas Iscariot, Simon's son, to betray him."...

In John there are no accounts of the casting out of devils by Christ or his apostles. On that subject there is no word. Possibly John had his doubts. In the fifth chapter of Acts we are told that the people brought the sick and those which were vexed with unclean spirits to the apostles, and the apostles healed them. Here again there is made a clear distinction between the sick and those possessed by devils. And in the eighth chapter we are told that "unclean spirits, crying with a loud voice, came out of them."

In the thirteen chapter Paul calls Elymas the child of the Devil, and in the sixteenth chapter an account is given of "a damsel possessed with a spirit of divination, who brought her masters much gain by soothsaying."

Paul and Silas, it would seem, cast out this spirit, and by reason of that suffered great persecution. In the nineteenth chapter certain vagabond Jews pronounced over those who had evil spirits the name of Jesus, and the evil spirits answered: "Jesus I know, and Paul I know, but who are ye? And the man in whom the evil spirit was leaped on them so that they fled naked and wounded." Paul, writing to the Corinthians, in the eighth chapter says: "I would not that ye should have fellowship with devils. Ye cannot drink the cup of the Lord and the cup of devils. Ye cannot be partakers of the Lord's table and the table of devils. Do we provoke the Lord to jealousy?"

In the eleventh chapter he says that long hair is the glory of woman, but that she ought to keep her head covered because of the angels. In those intellectual days people believed in what were called the Incubi and the Succubi. The Incubi were male angels and the Succubi were female angels, and according to the belief of that time nothing so attracted the Incubi as the beautiful hair of women, and for this reason Paul said that women should keep their heads covered. Paul calls the Devil the 'prince of the power of the air.'

So in Jude we are told "that Michael, the archangel, when contending with the devil he disputed about the body of Moses, durst not bring against him a railing accusation, but said, 'The Lord rebuke thee.'" Was this devil with whom Michael contended a personification of evil, or a poem, or a myth? In First Peter we are told to be sober, vigilant, "because your adversary, the Devil, as a roaring lion, walketh about, seeking whom lie may devour." Are people devoured by personifications or myths? Has an allegory an appetite, or is a poem a cannibal?

So in Ephesians we are warned not to give place to the Devil, and in the same book we are told: "Put on the whole armor of God, that ye may be able to stand against the wiles of the Devil." And in Hebrews it is said that "him that had the power of death- that is, the Devil;" showing that the Devil has the power of death. And in James it is said that if we resist the Devil he will flee from us; and in First John we are told that he that committeth sin is of the Devil, for the reason that the

THE DEVIL

Devil sinneth from the beginning; and we are also told that "for this purpose was the Son of God manifested, that he may destroy the works of the Devil."

No Devil- no Christ.

In Revelations, the insanest of all books, I find the following: "And there was war in heaven. Michael and his angels fought against the dragon, and the dragon fought and his angels, and prevailed not; neither was their place found any more in heaven. And the great dragon was cast out, that old serpent, called the Devil, and Satan, which deceiveth the whole world; he was cast out into the earth, and his angels were cast out with him. Therefore, rejoice, ye heavens, and ye that dwell in them. Woe to the inhabitants of the earth and of the sea; for the devil is come down unto you, having great wrath, because he knoweth that he hath but a short time."

From this it would appear that the Devil once lived in heaven, raised a rebellion, was defeated and cast out, and the inspired writer congratulates the angels that they are rid of him and commiserates us that we have him. In the twentieth chapter of Revelations is the following: "And I saw an angel come down from heaven, having the key of the bottomless pit and a great chain in his hand. And he laid hold on the dragon- that old serpent, which is the Devil and Satan- and bound him a thousand years, and cast him into the bottomless pit, and shut him up, and set a seal upon him, that he should deceive the nations no more till the thousand years should be fulfilled; and after he must be loosed a little season."

It is hard to understand how one could be confined in a pit without a bottom, and how a chain of iron could hold one in eternal fire, or what use there would be to lock a bottomless pit; but these are questions probably suggested by the Devil. We are further told that u when the thousand years are expired Satan shall be loosed out of his prison. "And the Devil was cast into the lake of fire and brimstone where the beast and the false prophet are, and shall be tormented day and night forever."

In the light of the passages that I have read we can clearly see what the writers of the New Testament believed. About this there can be no honest difference. If the gospels teach the existence of God- of Christ- they teach the existence of the Devil. If the Devil does not exist- if little devils do not enter the bodies of men- the New Testament maybe inspired, but it is not true. The early Christians proved that Christ was divine because he cast out devils. The evidence they offered was more absurd than the statement they sought to prove. They were like the old man who said that he saw a grindstone floating down the river. Some one said that a grindstone would not float. "Ah," said the old man, "but the one I saw had an iron crank in it."

Of course, I do not blame the authors of the Gospels. They lived in a superstitious age, at a time when Rumor was the historian, when Gossip corrected the "proof" and when everything was believed except the facts. The Apostles, like their fellows, believed in miracles and magic. Credulity was regarded as a virtue. The Rev. Mr. Parkhurst denounces the Apostles as worthless cravens. Certainly I do not agree with him. I think that they were good men. I do not believe that any one of them ever tried to reform Jerusalem on the Parkhurst plan. I admit that they honestly believed in devils- that they were credulous and superstitious. There is one story in the New Testament that illustrates my meaning.

In the fifth chapter of John is the following: "Now, there is at Jerusalem, by the sheep market, a pool, which is called in the Hebrew tongue 'Bethesda,' having five porches. In these lay a great multitude of impotent folk- of blind, halt, withered- waiting for the moving of the water. For an angel went down at a certain season into the pool and troubled the water; whosoever then first after the troubling of the water stepped in was made whole of whatsoever disease he had. And a certain man was there which had an infirmity thirty and eight years. When Jesus saw him lie and knew that he had been now a long time in that case, he saith unto him: 'Wilt thou be made whole?' The impotent man answered him: 'Sir, I have no man when the water is troubled to put me into the pool; but while I am coming another steppeth down before me.' Jesus saith unto him: 'Rise, take up thy bed and walk.' And immediately the man was made whole and took up his bed and walked."

Does any sensible human being now believe this story? Was the water of Bethesda troubled by an angel? Where did the angel come from? Where do angels live? Did the angel put medicine in the water- just enough to cure one? Did he put in different medicines for different diseases, or did he have a medicine, like those that are patented now, that cured all diseases just the same? Was the water troubled by an angel? Possibly, what apostles and theologians call an angel a scientist knows as carbonic acid gas. John does not say that the people thought the water was troubled by an angel, but he states it as a fact. And he tells us, also, as a fact, that the first invalid that got in the water after it had been troubled was cured of what disease he had. What is the evidence of John worth? Again I say that if the Devil does not exist the Gospels are not inspired. If devils do not exist Christ was either honestly mistaken, insane or an impostor.

If devils do not exist the Fall of Man is a mistake and the Atonement an absurdity. If devils do not exist hell becomes only a dream of revenge. Beneath the structure called 'Christianity' are four cornerstones- the Father, Son, Holy Ghost and Devil.

IV: THE EVIDENCE OF THE CHURCH

The Devil was Forced to Father the Failures op God.
All the fathers of the Church believed in devils. All the saints
won their crowns by overcoming devils. All the popes and
cardinals, bishops and priests, believed in devils. Most of their
time was occupied in fighting devils. The whole Catholic world,
from the lowest layman to the highest priest, believed in devils.
They proved the existence of devils by the New Testament. They
knew that these devils were citizens of hell. They knew that
Satan was their king. They knew that hell was made for the Devil
and his angels.

The founders of all the Protestant churches- the makers
of all the orthodox creeds- all the leading Protestant theologians,
from Luther to the president of Princeton College- were, and are,
firm believers in the Devil. All the great commentators believed
in the Devil as firmly as they did in God. Under the 'Scheme of
Salvation' the Devil was a necessity. Somebody had to be
responsible for the thorns and thistles, for the cruelties and
crimes. Somebody had to father the mistakes of God. The Devil
was the scapegoat of Jehovah. For hundreds of years, good,
honest, zealous Christians contended against the Devil. They
fought him day and night, and the thought that they had beaten
him gave to their dying lips the smile of victory.

For centuries the Church taught that the natural man was
totally depraved ; that he was by nature a child of the Devil, and
that new-born babes were tenanted by unclean spirits. As late as
the middle of the sixteenth century, every infant that was
baptized was, by that ceremony, freed from a devil. When the
holy water was applied the priest said: "I command thee, thou
unclean spirit, in the name of the Father, of the Son, and of the
Holy Ghost, that thou come out and depart from this infant,

whom our Lord Jesus Christ has vouchsafed to call to his holy baptism, to be made a member of his body, and of his holy congregation,"

At that time the fathers- the theologians, the commentators- agreed that unbaptized children, including those that were born dead, went to hell. And these same fathers- theologians and commentators- said: "God is love." These babes were pure as Pity's tears, innocent as their mother's loving smiles, and yet the makers of our creeds believed and taught that leering, unclean fiends inhabited their dimpled flesh. O, the unsearchable riches of Christianity!

For many centuries the church filled the world with devils- with malicious spirits that caused storm and tempest, disease, accident and death- that filled the night with visions of despair; with prophecies that drove the dreamers mad. These devils assumed a thousand forms- countless disguises in their efforts to capture souls and destroy the Church. They deceived sometimes the wisest and the best; made priests forget their vows. They melted virtue's snow in passion's fire, and in cunning ways entrapped and smirched the innocent and good. These devils gave witches and wizards their supernatural powers, and told them the secrets of the future.

Millions of men and women were destroyed because they had sold themselves to the Devil. At that time Christians really believed the New Testament. They knew it was the inspired word of God, and so believing, so knowing- as they thought- they became insane.

No man has genius enough to describe the agonies that have been inflicted on innocent men and women because of this absurd belief. How it darkened the mind, hardened the heart, and poisoned life! It made the Universe a madhouse presided over by an insane God.

Think! Why would a merciful God allow his children to be the victims of devils? Why would a decent God allow his worshipers to believe in devils, and by reason of that belief to persecute, torture and burn their fellow-men? Christians did not ask these questions. They believed the Bible; they had confidence in the words of Christ.

V: PERSONIFICATIONS OF EVIL

The Orthodox Ostrich Thrusts His Head into the Sand. Many of the clergy are now ashamed to say that they believe in devils. The belief has become ignorant and vulgar. They are ashamed of the lake of fire and brimstone. It is too savage. At the same time they do not wish to give up the inspiration of the Bible. They give new meanings to the inspired words. Now they say that devils were only personifications of evil. If the devils were only personifications of evil, what were the angels? Was the angel who told Joseph who the father of Christ was, a personification? Was the Holy Ghost only the personification of a father? Was the angel who told Joseph that Herod was dead a personification of news?

Were the angels who rolled away the stone and sat clothed in shining garments in the empty sepulcher of Christ a couple of personifications? Were all the angels described in the Old Testament imaginary shadows- bodiless personifications? If the angels of the Bible are real angels, the devils are real devils. Let us be honest with ourselves and each other and give to the Bible its natural, obvious meaning. Let us admit that the writers believed what they wrote. If we believe that they were mistaken, let us have the honesty and courage to say so. Certainly we have no right to change or avoid their meaning, or to dishonestly correct their mistakes. Timid preachers sully their own souls when they change what the writers of the Bible believed to be facts to allegories, parables, poems and myths. It is impossible for any man who believes in the inspiration of the Bible to explain away the Devil. If the Bible is true the Devil exists. There is no escape from this.

If the Devil does not exist the Bible is not true. There is no escape from this. I admit that the Devil of the Bible is an impossible contradiction; an impossible being. This Devil is the enemy of God and God is his. Now, why should this Devil, in another world, torment sinners, who are His friends, to please God, his enemy?

If the Devil is a personification, so is hell and the lake of fire and brimstone. All these horrors fade into allegories; into ignorant lies. Any clergyman who can read the Bible and then say that devils are personifications of evil is himself a personification of stupidity or hypocrisy.

THE DEVIL

VI

Does any intelligent man now, whose brain has not been deformed by superstition, believe in the existence of the Devil? What evidence have we that he exists? Where does this Devil live? What does he do for a livelihood? What does he eat? If he does not eat, he cannot think. He cannot think without the expenditure of force. He cannot create force; he must borrow it- that is to say, he must eat. How does he move from place to place? Does he walk or does he fly, or has he invented some machine? What object has he in life ? What idea of success? This Devil, according to the Bible, knows that he is to be defeated; knows that the end is absolute and eternal failure; knows that every step he takes leads to the infinite catastrophe. Why does he act as he does?

Our fathers thought that everything in this world came from some other realm ; that all ideas of right and wrong came from above; that conscience dropped from the clouds ; that the darkness was filled with imps from perdition, and the day with angels from heaven; that souls had been breathed into man by Jehovah.

What there is in this world that lives and breathes was produced here. Life was not imported. Mind is not an exotic. Of this planet man is a native. This world is his mother. The maker did not descend from the heavens. The maker was and is here. Matter and force in their countless forms, affinities and repulsions produced the living, breathing world. How can we account for devils? Is it possible that they creep into the bodies of men and swine? Do they stay in the stomach or brain, in the heart or liver? Are these devils immortal or do they multiply and die? Were they all created at the same time or did they spring from a single pair? If they are subject to death what becomes of them after death? Do they go to some other world, are they annihilated, or can they get to heaven by believing on Christ?

In the brain of science the devils have never lived. There you will find no goblins, ghosts, wraiths or imps- no witches, spooks or sorcerers. There the supernatural does not exist. No man of sense in the whole world believes in devils any more than he does in mermaids, vampires, gorgons, hydras, naiads, dryads, nymphs, fairies or the anthropophagi- any more than he does in the Fountain of Youth, the Philosopher's Stone, Perpetual Motion or Fiat Money. There is the same difference between religion and science that there is between a madhouse and a university- between a fortune teller and a mathematician- between emotion and philosophy- between guess and demonstration.

The devils have gone, and with them they have taken the miracles of Christ. They have carried away our Lord. They have taken away the inspiration of the Bible, and we are left in the darkness of nature without the consolation of hell. But let me ask the clergy a few questions: How did your Devil, who was at one time an angel of light, come to sin? There was no other devil to tempt him. He was in perfectly good society- in the company of God- of the Trinity. All of his associates were perfect. How did he fall? He knew that God was infinite, and yet he waged war against him and induced about a third of the angels to volunteer.

He knew that he could not succeed; knew that he would be defeated and cast out; knew that he was fighting for failure. Why was God so unpopular? Why were the angels so bad? According to the Christians, these angels were spirits. They had never been corrupted by flesh- by the passion of love. Why were they so wicked?

Why did God create those angels, knowing that they would rebel? Why did he deliberately sow the seeds of discord in heaven, knowing that he would cast them into the lake of eternal fire- knowing that for them he would create the eternal prison, whose dungeons would echo forever the sobs and shrieks of endless pain? How foolish is infinite wisdom! How malicious is mercy! How revengeful is boundless love!

Again, I say that no sensible man in all the world believes in devils. Why does God allow these devils to enjoy themselves at the expense of his ignorant children?

Why does he allow them to leave their prison?

Does he give them furloughs or tickets-of-leave?

Does he want his children misled and corrupted so that he can have the pleasure of damning their souls?

THE DEVIL

VII: THE MAN OF STRAW

Some of the preachers who have answered me say that I am fighting a man of straw. I am fighting the supernatural- the dogma of inspiration- the belief in devils- the atonement, salvation by faith- the forgiveness of sins and the savagery of eternal pain. I am fighting the absurd, the monstrous, the cruel. The ministers pretend that they have advanced- that they do not believe the things that I attack. In this they are not honest. Who is the 'man of straw?'

The man of straw is their master. In every orthodox pulpit stands this man of straw- stands beside the preacher- stands with a club, called a 'creed,' in his upraised hand. The shadow of this club falls athwart the open Bible- falls upon the preacher's brain, darkens the light of his reason and compels him to betray himself. The man of straw rules every sectarian school and college- every orthodox church. He is the censor who passes on every sermon. Now and then some minister puts a little sense in his discourse- tries to take a forward step. Down comes the club, and the man of straw demands an explanation- a retraction. If the minister takes it back- good. If he does not, he is brought to book. The man of straw put the plaster of silence on the lips of Prof. Briggs, and he was forced to leave the Church or remain dumb. The man of straw closed the mouth of Prof. Smith, and he has not opened it since.

The man of straw would not allow the Presbyterian creed to be changed. The man of straw took Father McGlynn by the collar, forced him to his knees, made him take back his words and ask forgiveness for having been abused. The man of straw pitched Prof. Swing out of the pulpit and drove the Rev. Mr. Thomas from the Methodist Church. Let me tell the orthodox ministers that they are trying to cover their retreat. You have given up the geology and astronomy of the Bible. You have admitted that its history is untrue. You are retreating still. You are giving up the dogma of inspiration; you have your doubts about the Flood and Babel; you have given up the witches and wizards; you are beginning to throw away the miraculous; you have killed the little devils, and in a little while you will murder the Devil himself.

In a few years you will take the Bible for what it is worth. The good and true will be treasured in the heart; the foolish, the infamous, will be thrown away. The man of straw will then be dead. Of course, the real old petrified, orthodox Christian will cling to the Devil. He expects to have all of his sins charged to the Devil, and at the same time he will be credited with all the virtues of Christ. Upon this showing on the books, upon this balance, he will be entitled to his halo and harp. What a glorious, what an equitable, transaction! The sorcerer Superstition changes debt to credit. He waves his wand, and he who deserves the tortures of hell receives an eternal reward.

But if a man lacks faith the scheme is exactly reversed. While in one case a soul is rewarded for the virtues of another, in the other case a soul is damned for the sins of another. This is justice when it blossoms in mercy. Beyond this idiocy cannot go.

VIII: KEEP THE DEVILS OUT OF CHILDREN

William Kingdon Clifford, one of the greatest men of this century, said: "If there is one lesson that history forces upon us in every page, it is this: Keep your children away from the priest, or he will make them the enemies of mankind." In every orthodox Sunday-school children are taught to believe in devils. Every little brain becomes a menagerie, filled with wild beasts from hell. The imagination is polluted with the deformed, the monstrous and malicious. To fill the minds of children with leering fiends- with mocking devils- is one of the meanest and basest of crimes. In these pious prisons- these divine dungeons- these Protestant and Catholic inquisitions- children are tortured with these cruel lies. Here they are taught that to really think is wicked; that to express your honest thought is blasphemy, and that to live a free and joyous life, depending on fact instead of faith, is the sin against the Holy Ghost. Children thus taught- thus corrupted and deformed- become the enemies of investigation- of progress. They are no longer true to themselves. They have lost the veracity of the soul. In the language of Prof. Clifford, "they are the enemies of the human race." So I say to all fathers and mothers, keep your children away from priests; away from orthodox Sunday-schools; away from the slaves of superstition. They will teach them to believe in the Devil; in hell; in the prison of God; in the eternal dungeon, where the souls of men are to suffer forever. These frightful things are a part of Christianity.

Take these lies from the creed and the whole scheme falls into shapeless ruin. This dogma of hell is the infinite of savagery- the dream of insane revenge. It makes God a wild beast- an infinite hyena. It makes Christ as merciless as the fangs of a viper. Save poor children from the pollution of this horror. Protect them from this infinite lie.

IX: CONCLUSION

I admit that there are many good and beautiful passages in the Old and New Testament; that from the lips of Christ dropped many pearls of kindness- of love. Every verse that is true and tender I treasure in my heart. Every thought, behind which is the tear of pity, I appreciate and love. But I cannot accept it all. Many utterances attributed to Christ shock my brain and heart. They are absurd and cruel. Take from the New Testament the infinite savagery, the shoreless malevolence of eternal pain, the absurdity of salvation by faith, the ignorant belief in the existence of devils, the immorality and cruelty of the Atonement, the doctrine of non-resistance that denies to virtue the right of self-defense, and how glorious it would be to know that the remainder is true! Compared with this knowledge, how everything else in nature would shrink and shrivel! What ecstasy it would be to know that God exists; that he is our father and that lie loves and cares for the children of men! To know that all the paths that human beings travel, turn and wind as they may, lead to the gates of stainless peace! How the heart would thrill and throb to know that Christ was the conqueror of Death; that at his grave the all-devouring monster was baffled and beaten forever; that from that moment the tomb became the door that opens on eternal life! To know this would change all sorrow into gladness.

Poverty, failure, disaster, defeat, power, place and wealth would become meaningless sounds. To take your babe upon your knee and say: "Mine and mine forever!" What joy! To clasp the woman you love in your arms and to know that she is yours and forever- yours though suns darken and constellations vanish! This is enough: To know that the loved and dead are not lost; that they still live and love and wait for you. To know that Christ dispelled the darkness of death and filled the grave with eternal light. To know this would be all that the heart could bear.

Beyond this joy cannot go. Beyond this there is no place for hope. How beautiful, how enchanting, Death would be! How we would long to see his fleshless skull! What rays of glory would stream from his sightless sockets, and how the heart would long for the touch of his stilling hand! The shroud would become a robe of glory, the funeral procession a harvest home, and the grave would mark the end of sorrow, the beginning of eternal joy.

And yet it were better far that all this should be false than that all of the New Testament should be true.

It is far better to have no heaven than to have heaven and hell; better to have no God than God and Devil; better to rest in eternal sleep than to be an angel and know that the others you love are suffering eternal pain; better to live a free and loving life- a life that ends forever at the grave- than to be an immortal slave.

THE END

31951076R00022

Made in the USA
Lexington, KY
26 February 2019